HELLO. YOUR PROMISE HAS BEEN EXTRACTED

Ahren Warner has published three collections with Bloodaxe Books. His first collection, *Confer* (2011), was a Poetry Book Society Recommendation and was shortlisted for both the Forward Prize for Best First Collection and Michael Murphy Memorial Prize 2013. He was awarded an Eric Gregory Award in 2010 and an Arts Foundation Fellowship in 2012. His second collection, *Pretty* (2013), was another Poetry Book Society Recommendation. His third collection, *Hello. Your promise has been extracted* (2017), is his third consecutive Poetry Book Society Recommendation. He is Poetry Editor of *Poetry London* and Vice Chancellor's Research Fellow at Loughborough University, and currently lives in London and Paris.

AHREN WARNER

HELLO. YOUR PROMISE HAS BEEN EXTRACTED

BLOODAXE BOOKS

ISBN: 978 1 78037 378 2

First published 2017 by
Bloodaxe Books Ltd
Eastburn
South Park
Hexham
Northumberland NE46 1BS

www.bloodaxebooks.com
For further information about Bloodaxe titles
please visit our website or write to
the above address for a catalogue.

Supported using public funding by
ARTS COUNCIL
ENGLAND

Printed in Great Britain by Bell & Bain Limited, Glasgow, Scotland, on
acid-free paper sourced from mills with FSC chain of custody certification.

You and I in a little toy shop
Buy a bag of balloons with the money we've got
Set them free at the break of dawn
Till one by one they were gone

NENA, *99 Red Balloons*

… Brueder, trinkt und stimmet ein,
Allen Suendern soll vergeben,
Und die Hoelle nicht mehr sein.

FRIEDRICH SCHILLER, *An die Freude*

HELLO.

Today, you will not go to the House of Terror.

And though each city east of Bremen bears the pockmarks of a bygone pogrom gouged into its brickwork

                     [though ghouls line the pavements and, tonight, the girl in the portico will hum as sadly sweet as ever, will rock her hips towards you, will keep her good eye turned towards her pimp]

                                  you will not push your index into, nor stroke the length of, a shrapnel-rent seam of render.

The bedspread is a bourgeois beige, your boxer shorts are mauve, your legs are threaded duck-egg blue.

There is a strong, pink gust hustling through the tilted window; the curtains – chocolate – stir and settle.

These are the facts, now take that idling finger tip and press it to the nub between your ribs.

There is a point, I promise, where the sternum splinters to trip the hinge of your own vertebrae on which your ribs will pivot open:

slow, unsure, and with the piglet's squeal of a rusted toolbox into which you can and must push your own fist.

Please, beat that putty mass of myocardium until it weeps, until its thick tears seep.

Please, go on.

This is the only way to go on.

HELLO.

What if you're neither spume nor froth and not, no, certainly not, the wave of history itself, but rather simple, reeking scum?

Imagine, please, the delightful and often desolate Iberian coast and, more particularly, that Northern stretch where slate cliffs and eucalyptus meet the grey Cantabrian Sea.

A small boy is standing on a black rock in an inlet near a village with no shops and one café run by a woman called Maria, as are all the women of this village and, indeed, the next.

Maria's husband snares lobsters for a living. Hence, the lobster scuttling on the bar, the same lobster – also called Maria – that Maria will one day bid you to caress.

It is unlikely that Maria has ever read Nerval. It is unlikely she is interested in the story you like to tell of him with a lobster on a gossamer thread. Very few people are.

A small boy is standing on a black rock with his small, tight pants around his ankles and his knob buffeted by the same Atlantic wind that spreads his piss into the air that overhangs the sea.

He is smiling. I repeat: what if you're neither spume nor froth and not, no, certainly not, the wave of history itself?

Some of the small boy's waz hangs in the perennial mist that threads its way between the high spindles of eucalyptus trees.

Some of it is carried out to sea. A little of it will wash up in a quaint cove at the foot of an escarpment on which a town sits stinking of the industrial production of milk.

It is possible, is it not, that you are not the wave of history, nor the ocean swell – dear Hegel's negativity – but a single piss-tainted bubble brought in on a sea-surge of others?

It is possible, is it not, that you are about to pop and leave nothing but the faint whiff of ammonia baking on a sea-mottled rock?

The rock, of course, will go on. As will the sea.

SOMEWHERE IN THE EYES, somewhere in the black bullseye
    of the pupil,
    you should find
white glass: Megablitz; bare incandescent; soft, atomic flare

of sunlight. There – in the photograph in which you are both
    voyeur
    and subject –
is neither sheen, nor crystal, nor screen, but black

within black. 'I saw my darkness,' he writes. Where light
    should trigger
    galvanic
fizz – soul, conscience – you stumble from black

to black. Outside, what remains of a cat – ragged fur,
    bones –
    sniffs at a bag
of shit. *If only you could wrench open your ribs.*

If only you could throw her your black, fat-skeined heart.

REMEMBER THE DARK. In Vienna, *Sekt*
fuelled,
your sour
tongue,
the stink of smoked
käse. A pan, girolles burned, butter turned
from brown
to black. Bats
swooned in the yard.

INTO THAT ALMOST GLADE, a hut, beyond the hut
black forest, needles dropped from high trees,

a faint, white river restless in the middle distance,
the door an almost mouth gouged between

chiselled shingle walls, a crevice or recess
into which you crawl, between two doors,

overlooking a road in which one journo
holds another journo bleeding out into

the sand, dirt, dry grass, a bullet lodged
for the night, cool air humming

between beech barks, stuttering to find
the dried trunk split like a dried carrot,

like elephant hide, like your heel
fissures and fills with mould, to find

the hole in which, short on gas,
short on men, filth for the shower

now scum running, now bullet splitting bone,
ce trou dans lequel on glisse une grande

langue – yes, uncommon cruelty, yes –
and you hunkered in a bamboo hut

and her running blistered, napalm
ridden, molten skin pooling on sand, dirt,

dry grass in which you lie, eyes fixed
between the slats of a black hut

in which he is, indeed, tied up,
bound to a rafter, wires running

from battery to wired balls, whitened
scrotal flesh where clips meet ball

sack in which they bung your mother
and fling her over into the Weise, Danube,

Vàm Cỏ Đông, Tigris, Rio Grande,
Rio Grande de San Miguel, the sack

in which they bung your mother
again and over again and fling her

over, singing: hour of danger, stern resolve,
wise and temperate harmony.

THE SKY IS SHUT PURPLE. Snow stains their hands. Adam and Eve get hot, noisy in the snow, on the lawn, all that is so often quiet. They are in their own coral mist, in too much light. God is righteous snow.

The artist studies the screen, jumps at the hand on his shoulder. It will snow. His face is infinite, his hands countless, these thousands of snowflakes sharper. Everything is snow: his brush, the smoke, trees.

Sometimes I see only my shoes drilling the whitewash. Blue lace, bright ochre, fine fabric, brown leaves of snow. The artist works in morning snow. The sky is a child running, laughing at me, pulling a large woollen scarf. No?

A digit or dactyl of snow, finger-tip
under the upper lip, needling until

a single lick of light hymns *ekstasis*.
Cut-glass light beyond the dacha,

birch trees, stone-white keloid skin.
Her leg, its stubble a small field

of smaller buds, white blossom, kasha.

HELLO.

Your promise has been extracted like the cow-horned remains of molars long-soused in a Diet Coke marinade.

You may not have felt it but, whilst you loitered or stopped to ponder some frozen splinter of the Danube playing host to blue-lipped skaters slinking on a waning gibbous moon,

we pulled the bastard out.

It's always possible, of course, that if you retake that path – if you find your own footsteps still frozen on Wagramer Straße and push yourself foot by foot into the once snug groove of snow-sheen – you'll find your way back

to a little blood, the odd gyzym of promissory pulp.

Though, more likely, you'll find yourself here, just off the Aldwych, where blue-lipped skaters slink against the fizz and blink of Our Lady of Employment Law, this year's sponsor, her animated billboard,

or

totally wrecked on Bow Street, retching your way past opera-goers, corporate *hôtes*, potentates of capital whose quaint tuxedos wear them as appendages, as hosts, as hernial *substantia*, on which their frayed existence holds.

Go home.

Go to your study to contemplate the scarf hanging behind the door and what a sturdy noose it would make.

Ape the scowl and twitch, the muttering to no one, those hallmarks of the only genius you've known.

Give yourself fully to each cerebral spasm: a raffle of pickled parts, the mother feeding on the flesh that she herself has bred, *les parfums frais comme des chairs d'enfants*.

Is there no when where this dream will rest?
    Blue smoke, wings, a plague
of walls, the city motionless, mass
    of mind and angst rising
in the brilliance of a cloudless light
    [*le ciel, c'est mauve comme la lavande*].

Everything turns in the quiet leisure of disaster:
    a kind of innocence
now supernatural darkness floating,
    trees shaking, waterways
swollen under a livid sky, storm clouds
    forming in the blink of an eye.

The thought of you is performative: blonde
        hair, pale complexion, downcast
jewels for eyes. Your dreadful martyrdom
        runs its course, written in mud
and butter: the human instant, in which
        you sing yourself full-throated.

Honey, ginger, flared saffron, grey-white
        momentous rhythm of sea,
barbarous smell of wet earth, ransacking
        or ravaged flowers, the landfill
site, shit-hole, killing ground from which we sup
        as shaking, hiccuping drunks.

To forfeit wisdom, atone for sins undone:
  the allegorical
hand thrust into torture, noise, shadows
  of men. Between the lines,
against the clock, this does not make,
   does not make a difference to them.

This age [*our* age] demands an image of its
  accelerated grimace –
an old bitch gone in the teeth, the ultimate
  cunt – our botched
civilisation, our grave in the sky: last jizz
  of consciousness.

I could have, now, blown my fucking brains out,
    but for a sweet shimmer of reason,
blood, lone bells in gritty belfries, the shallows
    of the sea, the surprise of days
which slide under sunlight, the soul
    gathered up, exhaled as rings of smoke.

Clay is the word and clay is the flesh. You
    drape your body against
my body, like a sheet of mirrored glass;
    you remain, comme *le dit*
Flaubert, melancholique devant son rêve accompli.
    – The word 'red' is not.

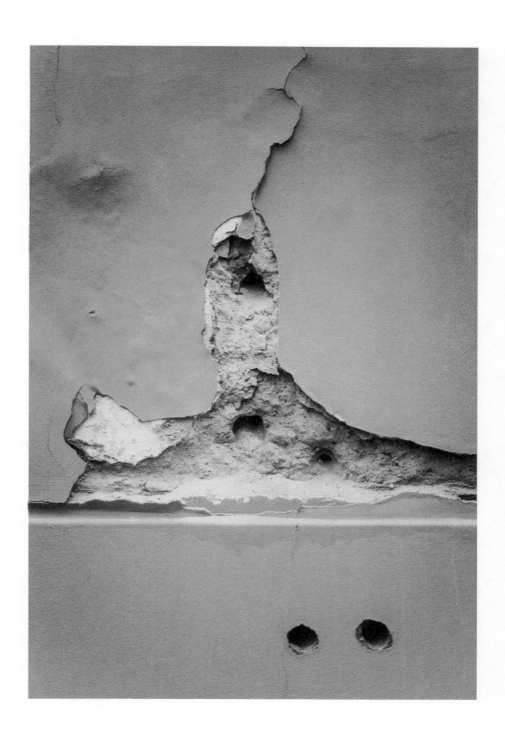

Forever in lust, forever in heat of fire and flood.
    Mule-bray, pig-grunt, bawdy
cackle and the stomping of feet to the beat
    of some undone family portrait
– bad teeth, bad eyes, beer and paint cans –
    the name and date split in soft slate.

Money makes an inverse difference
    to distance, when I lift her back
to me now: nothing there but that pale
    curly head working,
a machine up and down, an ochre
    autumn merging into twilight.

I read much of the night. Guns click and spit
    and split up timber, until
the river's tent is broken: old kettles, old
    bottles, a broken can, old iron,
old bones, old rags, that raving slut
    who kept the till.

Dreams nourished with tears, the sweet kinks
    of fists, light rain falling as mist.
The hours after you are gone are a lead
    white morning of hard, new ice,
the snow drift of that which is left unspoken.
    Care and great sadness are both a burden.

No gods, but a black swastika and no sky
     but grinding water, gasping
wind, the wares of carthage, girls
     with peacock eyes. The churn
of stale words staining the heart again:
     bleached wood massed as bones.

Your body is white as anemone petals,
     your skin is stone smooth, we
[as cold as the dead they load
     like a pile of baskets, mound
of refuse, the sweepings of a street]
     are pressed close together, swaying.

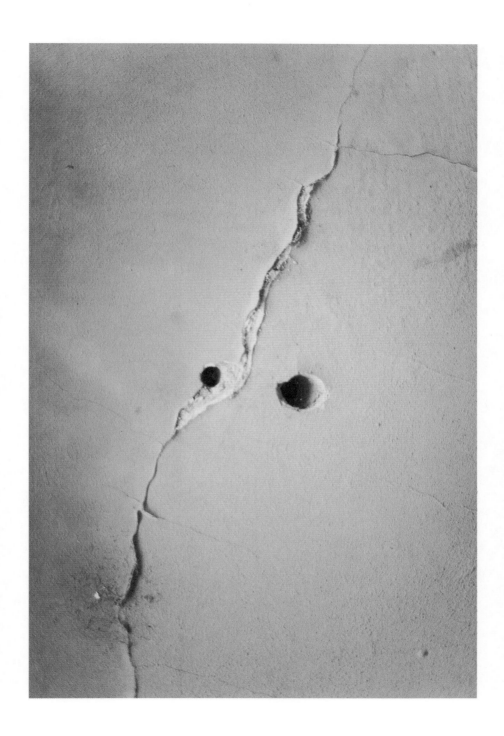

Merely the despaired occasion of wordshed
        made keener by blessed rage.
Scrape away the prison coating, the itchy sea;
        drink from this glass
of pure, real, resplendent blood, its
        malediction, freshly soiled and snug.

It's a question of altitude, probably, walking
        along your eyelid again, towards
your tear duct. This dance of fire
        that touches our lips, scorches
our tongues and pulls out the thin
        beaten tin of my squally voice.

O technosociety, where memory is tolerated,
        barely, as real estate
on which to mount steeples of rust, lay
        fresh mowed grass, burn gasoline:
anything so long as there's a margin
        and little but commerce between us.

We never have pure space in front of us, rather:
        slight bondage, the world's halter,
this fashion for dressing or setting our hair
        ablaze until we're ash and ash
in the heat of a blank but infinitely scrolling
        screen, flared back to scratch.

We begin and end with a groan, the tongue's
        comfortable wetness, sureness
of soul and fluttering lips. Then:
        lords of unquiet, quiet sojourn,
each atom which belongs to you
        belongs to me.

All abandoned, the last rig broken, the staggering
        shadows of trees, fence posts, gutted
cars, faces blurred and Sienese grave.
        I wish that I could speak only
of it all, the voices of children singing.
        A chapel, in spite of it all.

III

HELLO.

It's been suggested to me by some of those among you that a certain unrelenting doom might be a drag.

It's been suggested to me that we might take a break to dedicate a page or two to happy thoughts.

I've chosen ponies.

Please do not worry. I do not mean the kind that shift their feet against the dry remains of what might once have been the grass,

nor those whose bones creak and skulk beneath a flaking vellum canopy of rust.

Please, do not imagine a lame pony scuttling, wheeling against the ground, slated for retirement by Mr High-Velocity Rifle.

No, let us stick to the more generic kind, a much more cheery universal:

the Idea of the pony, devoid of all the grim particulars, e.g. the industrial supply-chain of frozen 'beef'.

I am thinking shades of hazy, pastel pink. I am thinking purple love hearts and frolicking pony manes,

the kind that turns us all to rosy puddles of love.

I want you to take this time for you.

I want you to give yourself permission, to give yourself the space to canter in the pony land of your own mind.

Are you done?

Good.

Outside there's work to do. Get heaving pony shit, black pudding, blood.

HUNGRY, violent, lonely, godless, thus sex: a sweetish point only for the wilted. For the lion-willed, wine of wines, a great fortifying: the laughing lion with a swarm of doves. Knowing is joy to the lion-willed. LOL.

Solemn, indeed solemn, worthy of a lion, or of a moral, howling, monkey. *Thou shalt* is the name of the grand dragon, but the lion says *I Will*.

Mottle-skinned, predator, mane of the explorer, searcher, conqueror, lion monster, grim, golden, blond-locked, gnawed off, nibbled away: SELAH

for the higher, stronger, more victorious, more cheerful ones: those who are built right-angled in body and soul.

Laughing lions
must.

THE GREAT BEAR IS IN THE CAGE
distracting himself with honey.

The great bear is in the sky
blue hurricane country.

Soup. Soup. Soup. Rage.
You will have nothing in your pot

but a broomstick and a pay cut,
a primate bride and an attic squat.

HOARSE FROM THE BADEST, badass cabaret of my octo-centenial performance, I – Saint Herbert – am checking out the pinstripe and tartan and tweed of the world's worst ice cream in a shop front on a northern esplanade.

I can smell gull shit.

I can feel the apocalypse.

It will rain, I am sure it will continue to rain. It will rain blood and locusts and flame, of course. It will rain formica; it is all rather exciting.

I *yearn* for marmalade.

It is written on Twitter that the sea is black, that the ducks are cooking in the lakes. It is written that every GIF is still. It is the end of historical time.

All around, architectural wonders are being pulled down by marsupials and the odd, terrible goose.

I can feel, let me tell you, my own lightness; the primacy of sound, the glory of my father, my own member: stiff as a slate and thumping.

WHEN IS TERROR NOT TERROR? When is terror
progress? Here, on Bessarabs'ka,

a beggar kneels, like beggars kneel
wherever. His head kisses a peel

of stone recovered from the snow;
he kneels on a sheet of filth that thaws

to a puddle of filth. Downriver, the river
freezes, Rodina–Mat rises, the Dneiper

is frozen mist, or the dry ice that capers
and flows around this salmon tartare,

this caviar, set here on a black, slate disc.
On Khreschatyk, you can buy anything:

just now a young, polite man asked me if
I'd like to buy a girl.

DOWNRIVER
STILL

in some cul-de-sac
of the Black Sea

the ghost

of a rusted hull
grunts
on a modest swell

its bodged seams
split
and spilling
kulaks.

Those not dead from thirst
or clubbed on their arrival somewhere;
those towed clear

those sunk.

And then
(again):

those with the strength to swim
those shot to shit
that sodden mass
of flesh become

sea-stain &
honeycomb.

YOUR MAN WENT FORTH AND WAS MOVED BY A
GREAT STARVING MULTITUDE.

Though – *sans les poissons, sans le pain*, only five
fretales to hand – his bleeding heart was moot to them.

Then, divine fury of angle-grinder spitting fire like
a small dyspeptic hound of hell.

Then, a dozen private hands with rasps, cold chisels,
hacksaws, working fissures of fretale like hell.

Then, a small, sacred mount of sharp slithers, frills
and filings growing to a Babel.

Thus: multitudes queued out the door, or would
have done if they were not in a desert place, were not a
Sabbath's day from the nearest door.

Thus: he thrust slivers of bronze down the mouths
of the needy in handfuls, bucketfuls, until the hungry,
malnourished, rattleboned, were full or overflowing.

O, how their lips and throats were shredded as lace
stained with maidens' hearts.

O, how the gurgle and gasp of the multitude rose
to one (endlessly catchy, endlessly bloody) *Amen*.

HELLO.

Please note the desperate ecstasy of the hag hunched in this shanty street is a ten-pence of kerosene, rat poison, carbonic acid and base shredding nerves and flenching flesh from bone.

Hag is the same age as Poppy, who you may have just helped bathe and dressed in a pretty dress and whose hand you might well hold all the way to ballet.

As we speak, there are boys of Poppy's age raping girls of Poppy's age in an orphanage in East Africa. Elsewhere too, obviously.

In many towns along the Niger, chemical fires are tended by ashen boys whose life expectancy is low.

Yes, to the annoyance of your neighbours, Arab orphans sleep outside your building. Have you noticed how their little hands snap like the claws of crabs at everything, even when it's handed to them?

Don't worry, this is not a con. I am not a student moonlighting with a bucket and a branded charity windbreaker attempting to pick your pocket with a little humour.

I know you care. I know the effort it takes to forget the river running between Tianjin and Beijing, the corruption of which is utterly complete.

I know the seam of guilt that opens between your lungs as you grasp the hand of the drunk hacking and idling his last few days on the street.

This is not a con, it's just a note to say I know you know the world's a writhing slaughterhouse of blood and garbage, infectious stink, disease and ruin.

Just a note to softly lull: you're right, there's nothing you can do — there's nothing to be done.

||||

I KNOW A TALL, narrow man who can enter a bar or café or slip into a gaggle engaged in conversation almost anywhere in the world and – although, in truth, he is forever uneasy – he never fails to appear at ease, to make conversation, friends.

I've watched him in a tea room in New York City, in a bar in Camden Town, in the front room of a chance acquaintance's two-up-two-down. I've seen how easily he slips from silence to interlocution. I've watched him hammered, his hands still nimble as he charms a whole bar with old card tricks.

He is a tall, narrow, innately social man.
I am not.

I am neither particularly tall, nor remotely narrow, nor gifted at small talk or brief, meaningful encounters.

This, perhaps, is one of the reasons that I find myself moved by the shimmy from rage to tears of a man in a café, here, on Eratosthenous.

Fuck the Germans
– his voice is a gash.

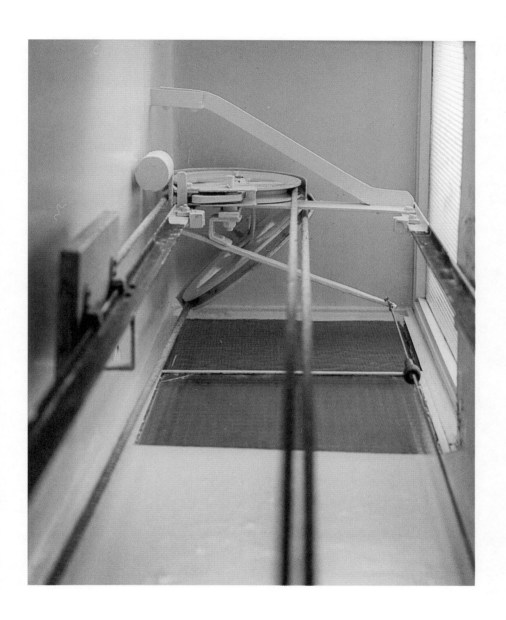

In truth, I am not particularly shocked by this man's animosity towards a country that friends of mine call home. A country in which I am often at home.

I am preoccupied with the fact of this man: a man who has served me coffee everyday for a week, a man for whom I have no name.

It is not, understand me, that I do not care. It is not that I do not want to know his name, or the name of his daughter. I am simply not very good at hurdling the moment in which one stretches out one's hand and mouths one's name as a question, as a demand for the intimacy of the everyday.

One night in Exarcheia, I am drinking with students and a colleague. One of the students of my colleague, a wealthy Greek American, is deeply concerned by our decision to drink in Exarcheia.

Years ago, two police shot a loud-mouthed unarmed fifteen-year-old dead two streets west of this café, riots followed, petrol bombs sailed through squares in Athens, then Thessaloniki and Komotini. Since then, I am told, the police do not enter Exarcheia.

I order ouzo. I have spent most of the week drinking something –
espresso freddo, Metaxa, ouzo – in Exarcheia.

It is true that studded anarchists doze and drink amongst the swings
of the central square, that their pitbull yawns and rolls and snores amongst
the municipal shrubbery.

On my first morning here – in a café on the square, having stumbled
across the district almost by accident – I am asked for a lighter by a girl
with a book. From behind, the girl's trousers flaunt four tiny stitches of
white thread below the waistband, announcing their four-figure price-tag.

Some months ago, the country's Finance Minister was jeered and threatened as he sat drinking here. I hear that on weekends black sedans sidle out from the side streets that join Exarcheia to Kolonaki, that their drivers open the rear doors for gilded youths to totter and sip among the unwashed, the anarchists, the poets.

So too in Kreuzberg and Neükolln, in Goncourt and Belleville, one finds kids from Charlottenburg and Neuilly sampling something they hope amounts to authenticity.

In *Aesthetic Theory*, Adorno tells us that by *crystallising in itself as something unique to itself, rather than complying with existing social norms and qualifying as 'socially useful'*, [art] *criticises society by merely existing*.

In the second series of *True Detective*, Colin Farrell mutters that *pain is inexhaustible. It's only people that get exhausted*.

On the first page of *The Inoperative Community*, Jean-Luc Nancy tells us that *the gravest and most painful testimony of the modern world... is the testimony of the dissolution, the dislocation, the conflagration of community*.

In Alexandré Kojeve's *Introduction to the Reading of Hegel* one reads that *history is the history of the working slave*.

As, day by day, the IMF, the EU, jack up their demands, here it seems that pain is inexhaustible. I do not know how many times I've been told that people are exhausted.

Half-cut and stuttering down Irodou Attikou, swinging the dregs of a bottle of ouzo, my path is blocked by a scrum of journos, a mess of mics and spotlights as the cabinet exit the Prime Minister's residence, each face a little sourer than the one before.

Hours before, I had been promised burlesque and charlie. Not, mind you, both together, rather burlesque *or* charlie: a choice of two different parties.

According to Kristeva's *Strangers to Ourselves*, the community can be defined as *a set that, by definition, comes into being by excluding the dissimilar.* As I rewrite this, from an armchair in Parmentier, hundreds are drowning off the shores of Athens, of Marseille, of Sicily and Almeria.

In Almeria, prostitutes whose bones jut like those of death-camp Jews, prostitutes with slash-scars from hip to hip, fellate and fuck for cash or junk. I know this because, in a small gallery east of Baixa, a man receives an award for their portraits.

| | | | |

Hello again.

May I invoke poetic licence? You're so young and not a little like a pedigree cat: coiffured fur, absurd ears, a memory that – but for the ecstasy of corduroy – sucks.

Do you remember, for example, that small beige living room with a grey TV, a packet of crisps, a slice of cheese, gawping as a jumbo jet parked itself in a tower, in a swell of flame, repeatedly?

Then there was that hot drive south in a small red car, a short stop in a lay-by near a village called Spittal as your lactose-intolerant friend tapped at his phone repeatedly

– his skin peeled away, his sister's whereabouts were unknown; the radio drip-fed explosions on the underground.

Of course, you may recall all of this. And yet, please write back:

Has it occurred to you that you were born at a false-dawn, spit-caked and toddling as the Wall tumbled down?

How do you feel that the distant pity you felt as a child for the severed limbs of children in Gikondo was a form of historical luxury?

In the fields between Johannesburg and Bloemfontein, angry white teens trample the flag and practise shooting blacks, repeatedly.

In the States, angry white cops shoot blacks repeatedly.

In Ukraine – soon forgotten for downed planes washed up on distant shores and the threat of hordes of walking corpses at the door – old powers settle back into their old ways.

By the by, in *your* country, the government is stacked with inbreds, incompetents who froth, who stiffen and swell at the chance to sell off what little of your future they can package into lots.

Do you sense you have lived very little but a lull?

Though you might not recognise it, history is here again.

EMPTY OF EVERYTHING BUT PURPOSE,
regular as breath, untenanted.

Pain, adrenaline ebbing, the floor
a pool of water, dabbed endlessly.

A strange, vague expansion
of the body: how smoothly you move

in the light blue of a low flame.
A strange, vague scene, many arms

extended, a door hung half off its top
hinge. The light: high, pure shining,

threading through your veins.
High screams, breathless.

Tiny stricken motions, the voice
gone high, cold like well water,

like so much vapour. The voice
falling as rain, as red fading to pink.

Burnt rubber, small face distended;
still in the pool, skull in the palm.

HERE'S THE THING, kitten: I love you.
And not in spite of, but in addition to
the sometimes disgust, often disdain,
I have for most of human-kind,
including several
of your own familial
line.

I love every treat of you:
from your toes
– which, it's true, I often feel
to be absurdly small –
to your nose, which is absolutely
neither pointy
nor redolent
of a young porpoise's snout.

So often, as you snore and snooze
like a stuporous dormouse,
I sob or putter:
your flesh is smooth as anti-matter
or the fur of a young camelid,
the radio hosts a dud
of a man informing us
of more atrocities,
by which he means a man
who watched his mother
being raped
placing his gun
on a child's lips
and pulling the trigger.

As children dallying under an oak tree, picking at acorns
        or waiting agog
as an ambulance stumbled across the playground

– as the sun splintered through bough or twigs,
        as the fields rolled past,
as one of us sobbed at his own, arterial gash –

we would angle and jut out our wrists, our tongues
        pushed under our lower lips
and turn to each other – to indicate to the other –

        that he was, indeed, a spaz.

        Here, amputations of course, deformity:
        hands balled as the paws of some sulking pug,

        the cup gripped in the hand that juts
        from the odd spastic wrist.

i.m. C K Williams

HELLO.

He's dead.

So, please go ahead: take the morning, these hours, for your own private grief.

It sucks, doesn't it? Of course, it's fine to have a little blubber, here, on the rue Lepic.

Though – given the cobbled streets, the accordion's musette, the tourists gawping wide and goofy eyed – it's all a bit absurd, isn't it?

Quand il y a tant de gens, tant de deuils, I guess you've got to choose and, of course, it's fine you've chosen him.

He was important, I know, he taught you how to think, he taught you that thinking isn't everything,

and yes, I know:

the lyre trilling blood, the poem as inveterate song sung below self-inflicted scars; that urge to hack and pick at mind.

But, have you looked outside? Almost everything's the same

and in some tenement, in the back room of some apartment hunkered in some crumbling edifice,

in some concrete grey monument to modernity and progress, someone else is dead

or dying, or about to boil a spoon of junk and flunk out of a world that never really noticed them.

So yes, he's dead.

It sucks, doesn't it?

it starts in rage not anger or rancour or a bitch cornered
whose fear-fuelled snarl turns fit nor the politesse of some
pale Ramón screaming

    no

    more of a jonesing more veins stretched as pig gut
over sphincter-mince more a thumbnail that breaks the
skin to pull a strip or length of rind to find

    neither

    plasma nor gristle nor bone nor the broken filigree
of nerves but pain that flares and fires like a fusilier gone
AWOL gone PTSD gone B.A.D. motherfucker

    a nail-bomb
    of rust and froth

    by which
    one means.

THIS MORNING, all is much
as before.

Though it is true that Nespresso has eased the torture
of self-caffeination,

that Buzzfeed has finally achieved
omnipresence.

Today: TEN THINGS YOU REALLY NEED
TO KNOW ABOUT THE AGONY OF AQUATIC SUFFOCATION.

Today: SMALLER PLANKS
REQUIRED FOR SMALLER CHILD'S *ULTRA* TINY COFFIN

will sell a few more papers
or snag a few more clicks

for editors weary *cum statu quo res erant ante bellum*,
e.g. mass graves, or the whole world in flames.

INDEX

ACKNOWLEDGEMENTS

Acknowledgements are due to the editors of the following publications, in which some of these poems have previously appeared: *Granta, New Boots and Pantisocracies* (Smokestack, 2016), *Ploughshares* (USA), *Φαρμακο* (translated by Lena Kallergi), *Poetry* (USA), *The New Humanist, The Poetry Review, Test Centre 6, Test Centre 7, Wild Court.*

Several poems in this book began in response to a residency at the Zoological Society of London, whilst another was commissioned by the Hatton Gallery/NCLA. I would like to gratefully acknowledge the support of the Society of Authors and the Royal Literary Fund for grants received in 2015 and 2016, and to acknowledge the support of Professor Linda Anderson and the Newcastle Centre for the Literary Arts for an appointment that gave me the time and impetus to write. Thanks too to the British Council in Athens, without whom parts of this book could not have been written.

Finally, and above all, big hugs to Messrs. Ching, Harsent, Irving, Phillipson & Waldron for their encouragement, invaluable criticism and support.